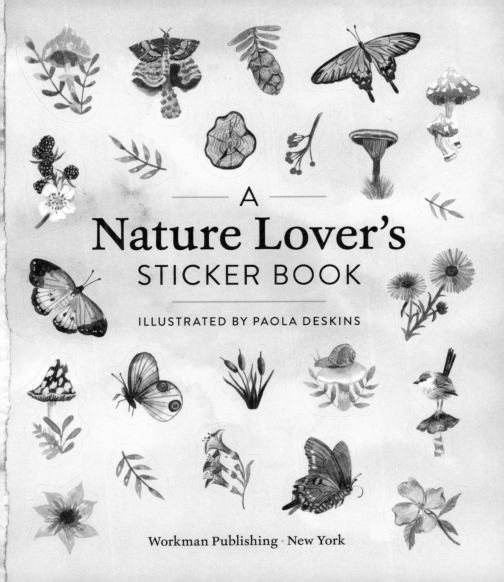

A
Nature Lover's
STICKER BOOK

ILLUSTRATED BY PAOLA DESKINS

Workman Publishing · New York

Workman
Workman Publishing
Hachette Book Group, Inc.
1290 Avenue of the Americas
New York, NY 10104
workman.com

Workman is an imprint of Workman Publishing, a division of Hachette Book Group, Inc. The Workman name and logo are registered trademarks of Hachette Book Group, Inc.

Cover design by Rae Ann Spitzenberger

The publisher is not responsible for websites (or their content) that are not owned by the publisher.

Workman books may be purchased in bulk for business, educational, or promotional use. For information, please contact your local bookseller or the Hachette Book Group Special Markets Department at special.markets@hbgusa.com.

ISBN 978-1-5235-2480-8

First Edition May 2024

Printed in China on responsibly sourced paper.

10 9 8 7 6 5 4 3 2 1

APPRECIATE ALL NATURE HAS TO OFFER
with lush and enchanting stickers! This book
is a visual love letter to the beauty of the world
around us, with 830 meticulously hand-painted
stickers that bring nature to life through delicate
brushstrokes and vibrant watercolors. Colorful
butterflies flit among blooming flowers; a curious
fox gazes into the depths of a sparkling lake; a
polar bear and her cub snuggle up for warmth.

For anyone who appreciates the wonders
of the natural world, these stickers are perfect
for adding a bit of whimsy and joy to journals,
letters, notebooks, postcards, and more. Let your
imagination roam free as you journey through
the pages ahead and find endless inspiration
in nature's bounty. There's so much magic to
discover in the great outdoors, if only you take
the time to look closely . . .

ABOUT THE ILLUSTRATOR

Every sticker in this book comes from the hand of Paola Deskins, the artist behind Pao's Art Nook. Paola's art often features animals, plants, and natural landscapes, inspired by her long walks outside. She considers nature to be her greatest teacher and her paintbrush the tool through which she learns its lessons. As an independent artist, she also accepts a variety of commissions. She lives with her husband and playful pup in Auburn, Alabama, where she enjoys hiking and appreciating the beauty of the outdoors. To see more of her work, visit paosartnook.com.